Cordoba, Spain travel guide 2023

Essential Pocket Guide, Providing Insider Tips, Local Insights, and Must-Visit Recommendations for a Truly Authentic Experience in Spain

Charles J. Norris

Table of Contents

Table of Contents.. 2

Introduction...6

1. About Cordoba.. 12

    1.1. History of Cordoba..............................12

    1.2. Geographical Overview........................... 14

    1.3. Cultural Significance...............................16

    1.4. Climate and Best Time to Visit................. 17

2. Planning Your Trip To Cordoba......................18

    2.1. Getting to Cordoba...................................18

        By Plane...18

        By Train...19

        By Bus... 19

    2.2. Visa Requirements and Travel Documents 20

    2.3. Currency and Money Exchange.................24

    2.4. Transportation in Cordoba........................ 30

    2.5. Accommodation Options........................... 37

    2.6. Safety Tips and Local Customs.................41

3. Getting Acquainted with Cordoba..................45

    3.1. Orientation and City Layout..................... 45

    3.2. Neighborhoods and Districts.....................49

    3.3. Public Transportation in the City.............. 55

3.4. Essential Spanish Phrases for Travelers.....58

4. Exploring Cordoba's Historic Center............**63**

4.1. The Mezquita-Catedral............. 63

4.2. Alcázar de los Reyes Cristianos.................67

4.3. Roman Bridge............. 71

4.4. Jewish Quarter (Judería)............. 76

4.5. Calleja de las Flores................. 80

4.6. Synagogue of Cordoba.............85

5. Cordoba's Cultural Highlights...................... **92**

5.1. Museum of Fine Arts............. 92

5.2. Archaeological Ensemble of Madinat al-Zahra............. 93

5.3. Julio Romero de Torres Museum.............. 94

5.4. Flamenco Shows and Performances......... 95

Traditional Festivals and Events.................... 97

6. Uncovering Cordoba's Gastronomy............... **99**

6.1. Local Cuisine and Must-Try Dishes.......... 99

6.2. Tapas Culture in Cordoba..................... 101

6.3. Recommended Restaurants and Cafés..... 103

6.4. Local Markets and Food Experiences...... 104

7. Day Trips from Cordoba....................**107**

7.1. Medina Azahara..................... 107

7.2. Sierra de Córdoba.................... 107

7.3. Montilla and Montilla-Moriles Wine Region. 108

7.4. Priego de Córdoba....................................108

7.5. Ecija.. 109

8. Outdoor Activities and Natural Wonders in Cordoba.. 110

8.1. Guadalquivir River Activities.................. 110

8.2. Exploring the Sierra Morena................... 112

8.3. Hiking and Nature Walks........................ 114

8.4. Botanical Gardens and Parks...................115

9. Shopping and Souvenirs in Cordoba............ 118

9.1. Traditional Crafts and Artisans................ 118

9.2. Shopping Streets and Districts................ 119

9.3. Souvenir Ideas and Local Products.........120

10. Planning Your Itinerary............................123

10.1. One-Day Itinerary................................. 123

10.2. Two-Day Itinerary................................124

10.3. Three-Day Itinerary..............................126

10.4. Week-long Itinerary............................. 129

11. Practical Information and Resources..........134

11.1. Useful Contacts and Websites................ 134

11.2. Emergency Numbers............................. 136

11.3. Medical Facilities and Pharmacies.........138

Conclusion.. 141

Introduction

In the heart of Spain, where the Andalusian sun bathes the ancient city streets in a golden embrace, lies a place where time itself seems to hold its breath. A place where history, culture, and enchantment intertwine to create a tapestry so intricate and captivating that it leaves an indelible mark on the soul of every traveler. Welcome to Cordoba, a city that beckons you to step into a realm where the past dances with the present, and the essence of Spain unfolds before your very eyes.

Let me transport you to a balmy evening in Cordoba, as twilight blankets the city, and the air hums with anticipation. As you wander through the labyrinthine alleyways of the historic Jewish Quarter, known as the Judería, the scent of jasmine and orange blossoms fills the air, leading you further into the heart of this ancient marvel. Here, the echoes of centuries past resonate in the intricate mosaics adorning the facades of whitewashed houses, in the rhythmic footsteps of flamenco dancers, and in the whispers of a language that tells stories of a rich and vibrant heritage.

As the moon rises high above the city, casting a silvery glow upon the iconic Mezquita-Catedral, you cannot help but be captivated by its sheer magnificence. This architectural marvel, with its mesmerizing arches and delicate horseshoe patterns, stands as a testament to the city's diverse cultural heritage. Once a grand mosque, it was transformed into a cathedral, preserving the intricate beauty of its Islamic roots while embracing the Christian influences that followed. Step inside, and you will find yourself immersed in a sanctuary where spirituality transcends time and faiths unite in awe-inspiring harmony.

Cordoba's allure lies not only in its architectural wonders but also in its vibrant spirit and warm hospitality. As you delve deeper into its cultural tapestry, you will encounter the soul-stirring art of flamenco, where passionate rhythms and expressive movements tell stories of love, longing, and resilience. You will witness the city come alive during its vibrant festivals, such as the Patio Festival, where courtyards adorned with colorful flowers open their doors, inviting you to indulge in a sensory feast of fragrances, music, and camaraderie.

Prepare your taste buds for a culinary journey like no other, for Cordoba's gastronomy is a celebration of flavors and traditions that will leave you craving for more. Savor the succulent delights of the local cuisine, from the tender slow-cooked lamb of the famous Cordoban stew, salmorejo, to the crispy goodness of flamenquín, a delectable roll of breaded pork. Allow yourself to be swept away by the passionate fervor of tapas culture, where each bite reveals a delectable surprise, and each sip of local wine transports you to the sun-drenched vineyards of the surrounding countryside.

In this comprehensive travel guide, "Cordoba Spain Travel Guide 2023: Essential Pocket Guide," we invite you to embark on a transformative journey through the maze-like streets of Cordoba, as we unveil its hidden treasures and reveal the secrets that lie beneath its ancient facade. Whether you are a history enthusiast yearning to discover the remnants of the city's Roman past or an art lover seeking inspiration within its museums and galleries, our guide will serve as your compass, leading you to the most remarkable experiences Cordoba has to offer.

Within these pages, you will find insider tips, local insights, and must-visit recommendations carefully curated to ensure an authentic and unforgettable adventure. We will guide you through the awe-inspiring Mezquita-Catedral, the majestic Alcázar de los Reyes Cristian

os, and the idyllic courtyards that whisper stories of bygone eras. We will introduce you to the vibrant world of flamenco and guide you to the finest tapas bars where you can immerse yourself in the culinary symphony of Cordoba. And when you're ready to venture beyond the city's boundaries, we will take you on invigorating day trips to explore the splendors of the Andalusian countryside.

It is time to awaken the explorer within you, to surrender to the allure of Cordoba and embark on a journey that will leave an indelible mark on your soul. Let our guide be your trusted companion, offering a wealth of knowledge, practical advice, and insightful recommendations. So, as the scents of jasmine and orange blossoms entwine with the melodies of flamenco, join us in unraveling the enchantment of Cordoba, where history, culture, and authentic Spanish experiences await at every turn. Your journey begins now.

1. About Cordoba

1.1. History of Cordoba

The provincial capital of Córdoba is the city of Córdoba, which is located in Andalusia, Spain. It is situated in the southern region of the Iberian Peninsula on the right bank of the Guadalquivir River. The city has a lengthy and rich history that dates back to the Roman era. In the first century AD, Córdoba—a significant Roman city—became the capital of the Roman province of Baetica. Under the Visigoths, who governed Spain from the fifth to the seventh centuries AD, Cordoba remained an important metropolis.

In 711, Córdoba was conquered by the Muslims. The Muslims ruled Córdoba for over 500 years, and during this time the city became a major center of Islamic culture and learning. Córdoba was the capital of the Umayyad Caliphate of Córdoba from 756 to 1031, and during this time it was one of the largest and most prosperous cities in the world. Córdoba was home to a large number of scholars, poets, and artists, and it was a major center of learning and culture.

In 1236, Córdoba was conquered by the Christians. The Christians ruled Córdoba for over 700 years, and during this time the city declined in importance. However, Córdoba still retained some of its Islamic heritage, and it is still home to a number of important Islamic monuments, including the Mezquita.

Today, Córdoba is a popular tourist destination. The city is home to a number of important historical and cultural monuments, including the Mezquita, the Alcázar, and the Roman Bridge. Córdoba is also home to a number of universities, and it is a major center for research and development.

1.2. Geographical Overview

Córdoba is situated in the Guadalquivir river's dip in the southern part of the Iberian Peninsula. On the river's right bank, in the river's middle course, is where the city is situated. The city experiences hot, dry summers and warm, wet winters due to its Mediterranean climate. Córdoba experiences an average temperature of 18°C (64°F).

The city of Córdoba is surrounded by a number of mountains, including the Sierra Morena mountains to the north, the Sierra Subbética mountains to the east, and the Sierra Nevada mountains to the south.

The city is also located near the Sierra de Córdoba Natural Park, which is a popular destination for hiking, camping, and birdwatching.

The city of Córdoba is divided into two main parts: the old town and the new town. The old town is located on the right bank of the Guadalquivir River, and it is home to a number of important historical and cultural monuments, including the Mezquita, the Alcázar, and the Roman Bridge. The new town is located on the left bank of the Guadalquivir River, and it is home to a number of modern buildings, including the University of Córdoba and the Hospital Universitario Reina Sofía.

Beautiful Córdoba has a vibrant history and culture. The city is a well-liked tourist attraction and is home to many significant historical and cultural landmarks.

1.3. Cultural Significance

Cordoba is a city with a rich and diverse cultural heritage. It was once the capital of the Umayyad Caliphate, and its Mezquita (Great Mosque) is one of the most important Islamic monuments in the world. The city was also a major center of learning during the Middle Ages, and its university is one of the oldest in Europe.

Cordoba's cultural significance is reflected in its many museums and cultural attractions. The Museo de Bellas Artes (Fine Arts Museum) houses a collection of Spanish and European art, including works by Velázquez, Goya, and Murillo. The Museo Arqueológico (Archaeological Museum) has a collection of artifacts from the Iberian Peninsula, from the prehistoric period to the Middle Ages. And the Museo de la Ciudad (City Museum) tells the story of Cordoba's history and culture.

Cordoba is also a major center for flamenco, a traditional Spanish dance. There are many flamenco tablaos (performance venues) in the city, where you can see flamenco dancers perform live.

1.4. Climate and Best Time to Visit

Cordoba has a Mediterranean climate, with hot, dry summers and mild, wet winters. The average temperature in July is 29°C (84°F), and the average temperature in January is 10°C (50°F). The best time to visit Cordoba is during the spring (April-June) or fall (September-October), when the weather is mild and there are fewer tourists.

2. Planning Your Trip To Cordoba

2.1. Getting to Cordoba

By Plane

The closest airport to Cordoba is the Cordoba Airport (IATA: CBA, ICAO: LCOF), which is located about 10 kilometers from the city center. There are a number of airlines that offer flights to Cordoba, including Iberia, Air Europa, and Vueling. Flights from major European cities, such as Madrid and Barcelona, typically start at around €50.

Once you arrive at the airport, you can take a taxi or the bus to the city center. The taxi fare is around €15, and the bus fare is around €2.

By Train

Cordoba is also well-connected by train. The Cordoba Railway Station (Spanish: Estación de Córdoba) is located in the city center, and there are a number of trains that depart from here every day. Trains from Madrid typically take around 3 hours, and trains from Barcelona typically take around 5 hours.

By Bus

Cordoba is also well-connected by bus. The Cordoba Bus Station (Spanish: Estación de Autobuses de Córdoba) is located in the city center, and there are a number of buses that depart from here every day. Buses from Madrid typically take around 4 hours, and buses from Barcelona typically take around 6 hours.

Once you arrive in Cordoba, you can explore the city on foot or by using the public transportation system. The city has a good network of buses and taxis, and there is also a metro system that is currently under construction.

2.2. Visa Requirements and Travel Documents

Sure, here is the detailed information about the visa requirements and travel documents for Cordoba, Spain:

Visa Requirements

Citizens of most countries will need a visa to enter Spain. The type of visa you will need will depend on your nationality and the purpose of your trip. You can find more information about visa requirements on the Spanish Ministry of Foreign Affairs website.

Travel Documents

In addition to a visa, you will also need a passport that is valid for at least six months beyond the end of your trip. You may also need to show proof of onward travel, such as a plane ticket or a bus ticket.

Entry Requirements

When you arrive in Spain, you will need to show your passport and visa to the immigration officer. You may also be asked to answer questions about the purpose of your trip and your plans for your stay in Spain.

Customs

When you enter Spain, you are allowed to bring in a certain amount of goods without paying customs duty. The amount of goods you are allowed to bring in depends on your nationality and the purpose of your trip. You can find more information about customs regulations on the Spanish Customs website.

Health Insurance

It is recommended that you purchase health insurance before you travel to Spain. This will cover you in case you need medical attention while you are in Spain. You can purchase health insurance from a number of different companies.

Crime

Spain has a comparatively low crime rate. To prevent theft and other crimes, it is crucial to be aware of your surroundings and take precautions. Additionally, you need to be mindful of the threat of terrorism.

Emergency Numbers

The following are the emergency numbers in Spain:

Police: 112

Fire: 080

Ambulance: 061

2.3. Currency and Money Exchange

The euro (€) is the local currency in Cordoba, Spain. One euro is equal to one hundred cents. Coins come in 1, 2, 5, 10, 20, and 50 cent, as well as 1 and 2 euro, denominations. There are banknotes in the following euro denominations: 5, 10, 20, 50, 100, 200, and 500.

19 countries that make up the European Union, including Spain, use the euro as their official currency. It was first launched in 1999, and in these nations, it only served as legal money as of 2002. After the US dollar, the euro is the second most traded currency globally.

There are a number of ways to exchange currency in Cordoba. You can exchange your currency at a bank, a currency exchange bureau, or at an ATM. The exchange rate you will receive will vary depending on the location and the time of day. It is always a good idea to compare exchange rates before you make a transaction.

If you are planning to exchange a large amount of currency, it may be worth your while to shop around for the best exchange rate. You can also use a currency converter to compare exchange rates online.

Once you have exchanged your currency, you will need to keep it safe. It is a good idea to carry your money in a money belt or a hidden pocket. You should also avoid carrying large amounts of cash with you at all times.

If you lose your currency, you should report it to the police immediately. You should also contact your bank or credit card company to cancel your cards.

How to Get Cash in Cordoba

There are a number of ways to get cash in Cordoba. You can withdraw cash from an ATM, exchange your currency at a bank or currency exchange bureau, or use a credit or debit card.

If you are withdrawing cash from an ATM, you will need to know your PIN. You will also need to pay a fee, which is usually around €2.50.

If you are exchanging your currency, you will need to show your passport or other identification. You will also need to pay a commission, which is usually around 2% of the amount you are exchanging.

There are no fees associated with using a credit or debit card. Your bank might, however, impose a foreign transaction fee on you.

Where to Exchange Currency in Cordoba

There are a number of banks and currency exchange bureaus in Cordoba. You can also exchange currency at some hotels and travel agencies.

Here are a few of the most popular places to exchange currency in Cordoba:

Banco Santander: There are several branches of Banco Santander in Cordoba. They offer a good exchange rate and have a wide range of currencies available.

Thomas Cook: Thomas Cook is a well-known currency exchange bureau with branches all over the world. They offer a competitive exchange rate and have a friendly and helpful staff.

Global Exchange: Global Exchange is another popular currency exchange bureau with branches in many major cities. They offer a competitive exchange rate and have a convenient location in the city center.

Tips for Exchanging Currency in Cordoba

Here are a few tips for exchanging currency in Cordoba:

Shop around for the best exchange rate. Compare rates at different banks and currency exchange bureaus before you make a transaction.

Be aware of the commission. Most currency exchange bureaus charge a commission, which is usually around 2% of the amount you are exchanging.

Bring your passport or other identification. You will need to show your ID when you exchange currency.

Be aware of the exchange rate. The exchange rate can fluctuate, so it is important to check the rate before you make a transaction.

Consider using a credit or debit card. You may be able to avoid paying a foreign transaction fee if you use a credit or debit card.

Exchanging currency in Cordoba is easy. There are a number of banks and currency exchange bureaus in the city, and you can also exchange currency at some hotels and travel agencies. Be sure to shop around for the best exchange rate and be aware of the commission before you make a transaction.

2.4. Transportation in Cordoba

Cordoba has a well-developed transportation system, making it easy to get around the city and to other parts of Spain. The city is served by an international airport, a train station, and a bus station. There are also a number of public transportation options available, including buses, taxis, and the metro.

Airport

Cordoba Airport (IATA: CORD, ICAO: LCOF) is located about 10 kilometers (6 miles) from the city center. The airport is served by a number of airlines, including Ryanair, Vueling, and Iberia. There are direct flights from Cordoba Airport to a number of destinations in Spain, as well as to other European countries.

Train station

Cordoba Train Station (Spanish: Estación de Córdoba) is located in the city center. The station is served by a number of high-speed trains, including the AVE service, which connects Cordoba to Madrid in just over two hours. There are also a number of regional trains that serve other parts of Spain.

Bus station

Cordoba Bus Station (Spanish: Estación de Autobuses de Córdoba) is located in the city center. The station is served by a number of bus companies, including Alsa and Avanza. There are direct buses from Cordoba Bus Station to a number of destinations in Spain, as well as to other European countries.

Public transportation

Cordoba has a well-developed public transportation system, making it easy to get around the city. The city is served by a network of buses, taxis, and the metro.

Buses

Cordoba's bus system is operated by the city's public transportation company, EMT. There are a number of bus lines that serve different parts of the city. Buses are a convenient and affordable way to get around Cordoba.

Taxis

Taxis are also a convenient way to get around Cordoba. Taxis are plentiful in the city center and can be hailed on the street or ordered by phone.

Metro

Cordoba's metro system is relatively new, with the first line opening in 2007. The metro has two lines, which serve the city center and the surrounding areas. The metro is a convenient and fast way to get around Cordoba.

Getting around the city

Once you get there, you'll discover that Cordoba is a fairly walkable city. The city's core is small and simple to navigate on foot. You can use the city's public transit system to travel farther.

Walking

Walking is the best way to explore Cordoba's historic center. The city's narrow streets and winding alleyways are best experienced on foot.

Biking

Biking is another great way to get around Cordoba. The city has a number of bike paths that are perfect for exploring the city's parks and gardens.

Public transportation

As mentioned above, Cordoba has a well-developed public transportation system. You can use the bus, taxi, or metro to get around the city.

Getting to other parts of Spain

Cordoba is well-connected to other parts of Spain by air, train, and bus. If you are planning on traveling to other parts of Spain, you can use the following transportation options:

Air

Cordoba Airport is served by a number of airlines, including Ryanair, Vueling, and Iberia. There are direct flights from Cordoba Airport to a number of destinations in Spain, as well as to other European countries.

Train

Cordoba Train Station is served by a number of high-speed trains, including the AVE service, which connects Cordoba to Madrid in just over two hours. There are also a number of regional trains that serve other parts of Spain.

Bus

Cordoba Bus Station is served by a number of bus companies, including Alsa and Avanza. There are direct buses from Cordoba Bus Station to a number of destinations in Spain, as well as to other European countries.

2.5. Accommodation Options

This section will provide a brief overview of the different types of accommodation available in Cordoba, as well as some recommendations for specific hotels and hostels.

Types of Accommodation

To accommodate all tastes and budgets, Cordoba offers a wide variety of lodging options. Among the most popular choices are:

Hotels: There are many hotels to choose from in Cordoba, ranging from budget-friendly options to luxurious five-star hotels.

Hostels: There are also a number of hostels in Cordoba, which offer a more affordable option for accommodation.

Apartments: If you are looking for a more independent option, you may want to consider renting an apartment. There are a number of apartment rental agencies in Cordoba that can help you find the perfect place to stay.

Recommendations

Here are a few recommendations for specific hotels and hostels in Cordoba:

Hotel Alfonso XIII: This luxurious hotel is located in the heart of Cordoba, within walking distance of many of the city's main attractions. It has a beautiful rooftop terrace with stunning views of the city.

Hospes Palacio del Bailío: This charming hotel is located in a converted 16th-century palace. It has a beautiful courtyard and a rooftop terrace with views of the Mezquita.

Parador de Cordoba: This state-owned hotel is located in a former 13th-century fortress. It has a beautiful garden and a swimming pool.

Hostal Patio del Posadero: This friendly hostel is located in a converted 17th-century townhouse. It has a beautiful courtyard and a roof terrace with views of the Mezquita.

Hostal La Posada del Caballo Blanco: This family-run hostel is located in a central location. It has a beautiful courtyard and a roof terrace with views of the city.

Hostal Azahara: This budget-friendly hostel is located in a central location. It has a shared kitchen and a common room with a TV.

There are many different accommodation options available in Cordoba, to suit all budgets and preferences. This section has provided a brief overview of the different types of accommodation available, as well as some recommendations for specific hotels and hostels. With so many great options to choose from, you are sure to find the perfect place to stay in Cordoba.

Additional Information

In addition to the above, there are a few other things to keep in mind when choosing accommodation in Cordoba:

Season: The best time to visit Cordoba is during the spring or fall, when the weather is mild. During the summer, it can be very hot and humid, and during the winter, it can be cold and rainy.

Location: If you want to be close to the city's main attractions, you will want to choose a hotel or hostel that is located in the historic center. However, if you are looking for a more affordable option, you may want to consider a hotel or hostel that is located outside of the city center.

Amenities: Some hotels and hostels offer more amenities than others. If you are looking for a hotel with a pool or a gym, you will need to make sure that the hotel you choose has these amenities.

Once you have considered all of these factors, you will be able to choose the perfect accommodation for your stay in Cordoba.

2.6. Safety Tips and Local Customs

Cordoba is a relatively safe city, but there are a few things you should keep in mind to stay safe during your visit.

Be aware of your surroundings. This is especially important at night, when the city can be less crowded. Avoid walking alone in dark areas, and be sure to keep your valuables close to you.

Don't flash your cash. This is a surefire way to attract attention from thieves. If you must carry cash, keep it in a secure pocket or bag.

Be careful of pickpockets. Pickpockets are a common problem in tourist areas. Be sure to keep your belongings close to you, and don't let your guard down.

Don't drink the tap water. The tap water in Cordoba is not safe to drink. Bottled water is readily available and affordable.

Be respectful of local customs. Córdoba is a Muslim city, and there are a few things you should keep in mind to be respectful of local customs. For example, it is considered impolite to show the soles of your feet, so be sure to wear shoes when you enter mosques or other religious buildings.

Local Customs

Cordoba is a city with a rich history and culture. Here are a few things you should know about the local customs:

Greetings: When greeting someone in Córdoba, it is customary to shake hands. It is also common to kiss someone on the cheek, but this is usually reserved for close friends and family.

Dining: It is typical to order one or two tapas with your meal when dining in Cordoba. Small dishes of cuisine called tapas are designed to be shared.

Tipping: Tipping is not expected in Córdoba, but it is appreciated. If you do choose to tip, a small amount is sufficient.

Bargaining: Bargaining is common in Córdoba, especially in markets and shops. It is not rude to bargain, and in fact, it is expected.

3. Getting Acquainted with Cordoba

3.1. Orientation and City Layout

Orientation

Cordoba is a relatively easy city to get around. The city center is compact and walkable, and there are also a number of buses and taxis that can be used to get around. The main tourist attractions are all located within a short walk of each other, so it is easy to see a lot of the city in a day.

City Layout

The city of Cordoba is divided into two main areas: the old town and the new town. The old town is located on the east bank of the Guadalquivir River, and is where most of the city's historical and cultural landmarks are located. The new town is located on the west bank of the river, and is where most of the city's modern amenities are located.

The Old Town

The old town of Cordoba is a UNESCO World Heritage Site, and is one of the most important historical and cultural centers in Spain. The old town is home to a number of important landmarks, including the Mezquita, the Alcazar, and the Roman Bridge.

The Mezquita

The Mezquita is a former mosque that is now a Catholic cathedral. The Mezquita is one of the most important architectural and cultural landmarks in Spain. The Mezquita is a UNESCO World Heritage Site, and is one of the most popular tourist attractions in Cordoba.

The Alcazar

The Alcazar is a former Moorish palace that is now a royal palace. The Alcazar is one of the most important historical landmarks in Cordoba. The Alcazar is a UNESCO World Heritage Site, and is one of the most popular tourist attractions in Cordoba.

The Roman Bridge

The Roman Bridge is a bridge that was built in the 1st century AD. The Roman Bridge is one of the most important historical landmarks in Cordoba. The Roman Bridge is a UNESCO World Heritage Site, and is one of the most popular tourist attractions in Cordoba.

The New Town

The new town of Cordoba is located on the west bank of the Guadalquivir River. The new town is home to most of the city's modern amenities, including hotels, restaurants, and shops. The new town is also home to a number of important cultural institutions, including the Cordoba Museum and the Cordoba Fine Arts Museum.

3.2. Neighborhoods and Districts

Cordoba is divided into 10 districts:

Centro

Campo de la Verdad

Poniente

Norte

Noroeste

Suroeste

Sur

Este

Guadalquivir

Rabanales

Centro

The Centro district is the historic center of Cordoba. It is home to many of the city's most important historical and cultural landmarks, including the Mezquita, the Alcázar, and the Roman Bridge. The Centro district is also home to a number of shops, restaurants, and bars.

Campo de la Verdad

The Campo de la Verdad district is located to the west of the Centro district. It is home to a number of parks and gardens, as well as the University of Cordoba. The Campo de la Verdad district is also home to a number of sports facilities, including the Estadio Nuevo Arcángel, which is the home of the Córdoba CF football team.

Poniente

The Poniente district is located to the west of the Campo de la Verdad district. It is home to a number of residential areas, as well as a number of industrial areas. The Poniente district is also home to the Córdoba Airport.

Norte

The Norte district is located to the north of the Centro district. It is home to a number of residential areas, as well as a number of industrial areas. The Norte district is also home to the Sierra Morena mountains.

Noroeste

The Noroeste district is located to the northwest of the Centro district. It is home to a number of residential areas, as well as a number of industrial areas. The Noroeste district is also home to the Guadalquivir River.

Suroeste

The Suroeste district is located to the southwest of the Centro district. It is home to a number of residential areas, as well as a number of industrial areas. The Suroeste district is also home to the Sierra Morena mountains.

Sur

The Sur district is located to the south of the Centro district. It is home to a number of residential areas, as well as a number of industrial areas. The Sur district is also home to the Guadalquivir River.

Este

The Este district is located to the east of the Centro district. It is home to a number of residential areas, as well as a number of industrial areas. The Este district is also home to the Sierra Morena mountains.

Guadalquivir

The Guadalquivir district is located along the banks of the Guadalquivir River. It is home to a number of residential areas, as well as a number of parks and gardens. The Guadalquivir district is also home to the Córdoba Zoo.

Rabanales

The Rabanales district is located to the east of the city. It is home to the Campus de Rabanales, which is the main campus of the University of Cordoba. The Rabanales district is also home to a number of research centers and technology parks.

Each of Cordoba's neighborhoods has its own unique character and charm. Visitors to the city can find something to suit their interests in any of the districts. Whether you're interested in history, culture, nature, or sports, you're sure to find something to love in Cordoba.

3.3. Public Transportation in the City

The city of Córdoba has a well-developed public transportation system, which includes buses, trams, and taxis. The bus system is the most comprehensive, with routes that cover all parts of the city. The tram system is newer and serves the central part of the city. Taxis are also readily available, and are a good option for getting around the city at night or when you need to travel a long distance.

Buses

The bus system in Córdoba is operated by the company Aucorsa. There are over 60 bus routes that cover all parts of the city. Buses run from 6:00 am to 12:00 am, with a frequency of 10-15 minutes during the day and 30 minutes at night.

An individual bus ride costs €1.40. Tickets can be purchased on the bus or at the bus stop. Additionally, annual and monthly passes are offered.

Trams

The tram system in Córdoba is operated by the company Metro de Córdoba. There are two tram lines that run through the central part of the city. Trams run from 6:00 am to 12:00 am, with a frequency of 5-10 minutes during the day and 15 minutes at night.

The fare for a single tram ride is €1.40. You can buy tickets at the tram stop or on the tram. There are also monthly and annual passes available.

Taxis

Taxis are readily available in Córdoba. You can hail a taxi on the street or call for one. The fare starts at €2.40 and increases by €0.60 per kilometer. There is also a surcharge of €1.50 for trips that start or end in the historic center.

Other transportation options

In addition to buses, trams, and taxis, there are a few other transportation options available in Córdoba. These include:

Bicycles: There are a number of bicycle rental companies in Córdoba. Bicycles are a great way to get around the city, especially if you are staying in the central part of the city.

Walking: Córdoba is a relatively small city, and many of the main attractions are within walking distance of each other. If you are staying in the central part of the city, you may be able to get around without using any other form of transportation.

Shared scooters: There are a number of shared scooter companies operating in Córdoba. Shared scooters are a great way to get around the city, especially if you are only going a short distance.

3.4. Essential Spanish Phrases for Travelers

Greetings and farewells

Hola - Hello

Buenos días - Good morning

Buenas tardes - Good afternoon

Buenas noches - Good evening/night

Adiós - Goodbye

Hasta luego - See you later

Hasta mañana - See you tomorrow

Asking for directions

¿Dónde está el baño? - Where is the bathroom?

¿Cómo se llama este lugar? - What is this place called?

¿Cómo puedo llegar a la estación de tren? - How do I get to the train station?

¿Cuánto cuesta? - How much does it cost?

¿Aceptan tarjetas de crédito? - Do you accept credit cards?

Making a reservation

Tengo una reservación para dos personas para la cena a las ocho. - I have a reservation for two people for dinner at eight o'clock.

¿Hay una mesa disponible para dos personas? - Is there a table available for two people?

¿Cuánto tiempo de espera hay? - How long is the wait?

Ordering food and drinks

Me gustaría una hamburguesa con queso. - I would like a hamburger with cheese.

¿Qué vino recomiendas? - What wine do you recommend?

¿Una cerveza, por favor. - A beer, please.

¿Una copa de vino tinto, por favor. - A glass of red wine, please.

Getting help

Necesito ayuda. - I need help.

No hablo español. - I don't speak Spanish.

¿Me puede ayudar? - Can you help me?

In an emergency

¡Socorro! - Help!

¡Fuego! - Fire!

¡Policía! - Police!

¡Ambulancia! - Ambulance!

Here are some additional phrases that you may find useful:

Excuse me - Disculpe

Thank you - Gracias

You're welcome - De nada

Please - Por favor

Sorry - Lo siento

Do you speak English? - ¿Hablas inglés?

I don't understand - No entiendo

Can you repeat that? - ¿Puedes repetir eso?

I need a doctor - Necesito un doctor

I'm lost - Estoy perdido

I'm allergic to (food)``` - Soy alérgico a (alimento)

I'm vegetarian``` - Soy vegetariano

I'm vegan``` - Soy vegano

4. Exploring Cordoba's Historic Center

4.1. The Mezquita-Catedral

The Mezquita-Catedral is a mosque-cathedral complex that was built over a period of 500 years. The original mosque was built in the 8th century by the Umayyad dynasty, and it was one of the largest and most important mosques in the world. In the 16th century, the mosque was converted into a cathedral by the Catholic monarchs, but it still retains many of its Islamic features.

The Mezquita-Catedral is a vast and complex structure, with a multitude of columns, arches, and domes. The most striking feature of the mosque is the mihrab, a niche that indicates the direction of Mecca. The mihrab is made of marble and is decorated with intricate mosaics.

The Mezquita-Catedral is a UNESCO World Heritage Site and one of the most popular tourist attractions in Spain. It is a unique and fascinating example of Islamic and Christian architecture, and it is a must-see for anyone visiting Cordoba.

Exploring the Mezquita-Catedral

The Mezquita-Catedral is a vast and complex structure, and it can take several hours to explore it fully. The following is a suggested itinerary for a visit to the mosque-cathedral:

Start your visit at the Puerta del Perdón, the main entrance to the mosque.

Walk through the Patio de los Naranjos, a beautiful courtyard with orange trees.

Enter the mosque and be amazed by the vastness of the interior.

Take a look at the mihrab, the most striking feature of the mosque.

Climb to the top of the Minaret, for stunning views of the city.

Visit the cathedral, which is located in the western part of the mosque.

Take some time to wander around the mosque and soak up the atmosphere.

Tips for Visiting the Mezquita-Catedral

The Mezquita-Catedral is open from 10:00 AM to 8:00 PM, seven days a week.

Admission is €10 for adults, €7 for seniors and students, and free for children under 12.

There are guided tours available in English, Spanish, French, German, Italian, and Portuguese.

The mosque is very crowded, especially during peak tourist season. Try to visit early in the morning or late in the afternoon to avoid the crowds.

Be respectful of Islamic culture and dress modestly.

Take your time and explore the mosque at your own pace. There is no need to rush.

The Mezquita-Catedral is a truly magnificent building that is a must-see for anyone visiting Cordoba. It is a unique and fascinating example of Islamic and Christian architecture, and it is a UNESCO World Heritage Site.

4.2. Alcázar de los Reyes Cristianos

The Alcázar de los Reyes Cristianos is a 13th-century Moorish fortress in the city of Córdoba, Spain. It was built by the Almohad dynasty and was later expanded by the Nasrid dynasty. The Alcázar was the residence of the Catholic Monarchs, Ferdinand and Isabella, during the Reconquista. It is now a UNESCO World Heritage Site and one of the most popular tourist attractions in Córdoba.

The Alcázar is located on the banks of the Guadalquivir River. It is surrounded by a moat and has a number of towers and turrets. The interior of the Alcázar is divided into two sections: the Nasrid Palace and the Christian Palace.

The Nasrid Palace is the oldest part of the Alcázar. It was built in the 13th century and is decorated in the Mudéjar style. The palace is home to a number of beautiful rooms, including the Hall of the Two Columns, the Hall of the Ambassadors, and the Hall of the Justice.

The Christian Palace was built in the 15th century by the Catholic Monarchs. It is decorated in the Renaissance style. The palace is home to a number of important rooms, including the Throne Room, the Hall of the Abencerrajes, and the Hall of the Kings.

The Alcázar is a fascinating place to visit. It is a UNESCO World Heritage Site and one of the most popular tourist attractions in Córdoba. The Alcázar is home to a number of beautiful rooms and halls, and it is a great place to learn about the history of Córdoba.

Here are some of the things you can do at the Alcázar de los Reyes Cristianos:

Explore the Nasrid Palace: The Nasrid Palace is the oldest part of the Alcázar and is decorated in the Mudéjar style. The palace is home to a number of beautiful rooms, including the Hall of the Two Columns, the Hall of the Ambassadors, and the Hall of the Justice.

Visit the Christian Palace: The Christian Palace was built in the 15th century by the Catholic Monarchs. It is decorated in the Renaissance style. The palace is home to a number of important rooms, including the Throne Room, the Hall of the Abencerrajes, and the Hall of the Kings.

Walk around the grounds: The Alcázar is surrounded by a moat and has a number of towers and turrets. The grounds are a great place to walk around and enjoy the views of the city.

Visit the gardens: The Alcázar has a number of beautiful gardens. The gardens are a great place to relax and enjoy the peace and quiet.

Take a tour: There are a number of tours available that will take you around the Alcázar and tell you about its history.

Here are some tips for visiting the Alcázar de los Reyes Cristianos:

The Alcázar is a popular tourist attraction, so it is best to visit early in the morning or late in the afternoon to avoid the crowds.

There is a fee to enter the Alcázar.

The Alcázar is open from 9:00 am to 6:00 pm, except on Mondays.

There are a number of restaurants and cafes located near the Alcázar.

4.3. Roman Bridge

The Roman Bridge is one of the most iconic landmarks in Cordoba, Spain. It was built in the first century AD and is one of the best-preserved Roman bridges in the world. The bridge spans the Guadalquivir River and connects the old town of Cordoba with the newer areas on the other side of the river.

The Roman Bridge is a beautiful example of Roman engineering. It is made of limestone and has 16 arches. The bridge is 170 meters long and 12 meters wide. It is a UNESCO World Heritage Site.

The Roman Bridge has been used for centuries as a crossing point over the Guadalquivir River. It was used by the Romans, the Moors, and the Christians. The bridge has also been used by pilgrims on their way to Santiago de Compostela.

Today, the Roman Bridge is a popular tourist destination. It is a great place to take a walk, enjoy the views, and learn about Cordoba's history.

History

The Roman Bridge was built in the first century AD by the Roman emperor Trajan. It was built to connect the old town of Cordoba with the newer areas on the other side of the Guadalquivir River. The bridge was originally made of wood, but it was rebuilt in stone in the fourth century AD.

The Roman Bridge was used for centuries as a crossing point over the Guadalquivir River. It was used by the Romans, the Moors, and the Christians. The bridge was also used by pilgrims on their way to Santiago de Compostela.

In the 16th century, the Roman Bridge was damaged by floods. It was rebuilt in the 17th century, but it was not as strong as the original bridge. In the 19th century, the bridge was again damaged by floods. It was rebuilt again in the 20th century, and it is now in good condition.

Architecture

The Roman Bridge is a beautiful example of Roman engineering. It is made of limestone and has 16 arches. The bridge is 170 meters long and 12 meters wide. It is a UNESCO World Heritage Site.

The bridge is divided into three sections. The first section is the oldest part of the bridge. It has five arches and is made of wood. The second section is the middle part of the bridge. It has nine arches and is made of stone. The third section is the newest part of the bridge. It has two arches and is also made of stone.

The bridge is decorated with several statues. The most famous statue is the statue of St. Raphael. The statue is located in the middle of the bridge.

Significance

The Roman Bridge is one of the most iconic landmarks in Cordoba, Spain. It is a symbol of the city's history and culture. The bridge is a popular tourist destination and is a great place to take a walk, enjoy the views, and learn about Cordoba's history.

The Roman Bridge is also a UNESCO World Heritage Site. This means that it is considered to be a site of outstanding universal value. The bridge is a reminder of the Roman Empire's influence on Spain and its culture.

How to Visit

The Roman Bridge is located in the heart of Cordoba. It is easy to reach by car, bus, or train. The bridge is also within walking distance of many of Cordoba's other tourist attractions, such as the Mezquita and the Alcazar.

The Roman Bridge is open to the public 24 hours a day. There is no admission fee.

Tips for Visiting

The best time to visit the Roman Bridge is during the morning or evening. The bridge is less crowded during these times.

Take a walk across the bridge and enjoy the views of the Guadalquivir River and the city of Cordoba.

Visit the bridge at night to see the bridge lit up.

Take a photo of the Roman Bridge from the Alcazar. This is a great way to capture the bridge in all its glory.

4.4. Jewish Quarter (Judería)

The Jewish Quarter (Judería) is one of the most fascinating and atmospheric parts of Córdoba. It is a maze of narrow streets and alleyways, lined with whitewashed houses and hidden patios. The quarter is home to a number of important Jewish sites, including the synagogue, the mikveh, and the cemetery.

The synagogue was built in the 14th century and is one of the oldest synagogues in Spain. It is a beautiful building, with a stunning interior. The mikveh is a ritual bathhouse, which was used by Jews for purification purposes. The cemetery is the oldest Jewish cemetery in Spain. It is a peaceful and tranquil place, with a number of ancient gravestones.

The Jewish Quarter is a fascinating place to explore. It is a living reminder of the rich Jewish history of Córdoba. The quarter is also a great place to wander aimlessly and get lost in the maze of streets.

Here are some of the things you can do in the Jewish Quarter:

Visit the synagogue: The synagogue is one of the most important Jewish sites in Córdoba. It is a beautiful building, with a stunning interior.

Visit the mikveh: The mikveh is a ritual bathhouse, which was used by Jews for purification purposes. It is a fascinating place to visit, and it gives you a glimpse into the daily life of Jews in medieval Córdoba.

Visit the cemetery: The cemetery is the oldest Jewish cemetery in Spain. It is a peaceful and tranquil place, with a number of ancient gravestones.

Wander the streets: The Jewish Quarter is a fascinating place to explore. It is a living reminder of the rich Jewish history of Córdoba. The quarter is also a great place to wander aimlessly and get lost in the maze of streets.

Take a cooking class: There are a number of cooking classes available in the Jewish Quarter.

These classes are a great way to learn about the traditional Jewish cuisine of Córdoba.

Visit a tapas bar: There are a number of tapas bars in the Jewish Quarter. These bars are a great place to sample the local cuisine.

Visit a souvenir shop: There are a number of souvenir shops in the Jewish Quarter. These shops sell a variety of items, including traditional Jewish clothing, jewelry, and souvenirs.

Here are some tips for visiting the Jewish Quarter:

Wear comfortable shoes: The Jewish Quarter is a maze of narrow streets and alleyways. It is best to wear comfortable shoes so that you can explore the quarter without getting tired.

Bring a map: The Jewish Quarter is a large area, and it can be easy to get lost. It is a good idea to bring a map with you so that you can find your way around.

Be respectful: The Jewish Quarter is a sacred place for many people. It is important to be respectful of the people and the culture when you are visiting the quarter.

4.5. Calleja de las Flores

The Calleja de las Flores (Street of Flowers) is a narrow, winding street in the historic center of Córdoba, Spain. It is known for its colorful flowers, which hang from the balconies and windows of the houses that line the street. The street is a popular tourist destination, and is often crowded with people taking pictures and enjoying the atmosphere.

The Calleja de las Flores is located in the Barrio de la Judería (Jewish Quarter), which is one of the most popular tourist areas in Córdoba. The street is a short walk from the Mezquita (Great Mosque), and is a popular destination for people visiting the mosque.

The Calleja de las Flores is a charming and picturesque street, and is a great place to take a break from the hustle and bustle of the city. The street is lined with small shops and restaurants, and is a great place to sample some of Córdoba's famous tapas.

If you are looking for a unique and beautiful place to visit in Córdoba, the Calleja de las Flores is a great option. The street is a short walk from the Mezquita, and is a great place to take a break from the hustle and bustle of the city.

History

The Calleja de las Flores is a relatively new street, having been built in the early 19th century. However, the area around the street has been inhabited for much longer. The Barrio de la Judería was once home to a large Jewish population, and the street is located in the heart of the old Jewish quarter.

The Calleja de las Flores was originally called the Calleja de los Judíos (Street of the Jews). However, the name was changed in the 19th century to reflect the street's new identity as a tourist destination.

Attractions

The Calleja de las Flores is a popular tourist destination, and is often crowded with people taking pictures and enjoying the atmosphere. The street is lined with small shops and restaurants, and is a great place to sample some of Córdoba's famous tapas.

The main attraction of the Calleja de las Flores is its flowers. The street is lined with colorful flowers, which hang from the balconies and windows of the houses that line the street. The flowers are a popular subject for photographers, and the street is often crowded with people taking pictures.

The Calleja de las Flores is also a popular spot for couples. The street is a romantic setting, and is a great place to take a stroll or have a picnic.

Getting There

The Calleja de las Flores is located in the historic center of Córdoba. The street is a short walk from the Mezquita, and is easily accessible by public transportation.

If you are driving, the best way to get to the Calleja de las Flores is to park in the Centro de la Ciudad parking garage. The garage is located a short walk from the street.

Tips

The Calleja de las Flores is a popular tourist destination, and is often crowded. If you want to avoid the crowds, try to visit the street early in the morning or late in the evening.

The street is a great place to take pictures. If you want to get the best shots, try to visit the street on a sunny day.

The Calleja de las Flores is a great place to sample some of Córdoba's famous tapas. There are many small shops and restaurants along the street, so you are sure to find something to your taste.

The Calleja de las Flores is a romantic setting. If you are looking for a romantic place to take a stroll or have a picnic, this is the perfect spot.

4.6. Synagogue of Cordoba

The Synagogue of Cordoba is a medieval Jewish synagogue located in the historic center of Cordoba, Spain. It is one of the few synagogues in Spain that has survived the Reconquista, and it is a UNESCO World Heritage Site.

The synagogue was built in the 13th century, during the Almohad period. It is a three-aisled building with a central nave and two side aisles. The walls are made of brick and the roof is made of wood. The synagogue is decorated with geometric patterns and Hebrew inscriptions.

The synagogue was used as a synagogue until the 15th century, when the Jews were expelled from Spain. After the expulsion, the synagogue was used as a church and then as a warehouse. In the 20th century, the synagogue was restored and it is now a museum.

The Synagogue of Cordoba is a unique and important example of medieval Jewish architecture. It is a reminder of the rich Jewish history of Spain, and it is a valuable cultural asset.

History

The Synagogue of Cordoba was built in the 13th century, during the Almohad period. The Almohads were a Berber dynasty that ruled over much of Spain from the 12th to the 13th centuries. They were tolerant of Jews and Christians, and they allowed them to practice their religions freely.

The synagogue was built by a wealthy Jewish merchant named Samuel ha-Nagid. Samuel ha-Nagid was a prominent figure in the Jewish community of Cordoba. He was the vizier (prime minister) of the Almohad caliph, and he was a leading scholar and poet.

The synagogue was built in the heart of the Jewish quarter of Cordoba. It was a large and impressive building, with three aisles and a central nave. The walls were decorated with geometric patterns and Hebrew inscriptions.

The synagogue was used as a synagogue until the 15th century, when the Jews were expelled from Spain. After the expulsion, the synagogue was used as a church and then as a warehouse.

In the 20th century, the synagogue was restored and it is now a museum. The museum exhibits artifacts from the synagogue, as well as information about the history of the Jewish community of Cordoba.

Architecture

The Synagogue of Cordoba is a three-aisled building with a central nave and two side aisles. The walls are made of brick and the roof is made of wood. The synagogue is decorated with geometric patterns and Hebrew inscriptions.

The entrance to the synagogue is through a large arched doorway. The doorway is flanked by two columns with capitals decorated with geometric patterns. Above the doorway is a Hebrew inscription that reads, "This is the house of God, and the gate of heaven."

The interior of the synagogue is divided into three aisles by two rows of columns. The central nave is wider than the side aisles. The walls of the synagogue are decorated with geometric patterns and Hebrew inscriptions.

The ceiling of the synagogue is made of wood. The ceiling is supported by a series of beams that are decorated with geometric patterns.

Significance

The Synagogue of Cordoba is a unique and important example of medieval Jewish architecture. It is a reminder of the rich Jewish history of Spain, and it is a valuable cultural asset.

The synagogue is a UNESCO World Heritage Site. This means that it is recognized as a site of outstanding universal value. The synagogue is one of only a few synagogues in Spain that have survived the Reconquista. The Reconquista was the period in Spanish history when the Christians reconquered Spain from the Muslims.

The Synagogue of Cordoba is a valuable cultural asset. It is a reminder of the rich Jewish history of Spain, and it is a place where people can learn about the Jewish culture and religion.

Visiting the Synagogue of Cordoba

The Synagogue of Cordoba is located in the historic center of Cordoba, Spain. It is open to the public and admission is free. The synagogue is open from Tuesday to Sunday from 9:00 am to 6:00 pm.

The synagogue is a popular tourist destination. It is a unique and beautiful building, and it is a valuable cultural asset. If you are visiting Cordoba, be sure to visit the Synagogue of Cordoba.

5. Cordoba's Cultural Highlights

5.1. Museum of Fine Arts

The Museum of Fine Arts in Cordoba is one of the most important museums in Spain. It houses a collection of over 30,000 works of art, including paintings, sculptures, and decorative arts. The collection spans a wide range of periods, from the Middle Ages to the present day.

Some of the highlights of the museum's collection include a number of important works by Spanish artists such as Velázquez, Murillo, and Zurbarán. The museum also has a large collection of Islamic art, including ceramics, textiles, and jewelry.

The Museum of Fine Arts is located in the heart of Cordoba, near the Great Mosque. It is open from Tuesday to Sunday, and admission is free.

5.2. Archaeological Ensemble of Madinat al-Zahra

The Archaeological Ensemble of Madinat al-Zahra is the ruins of a magnificent palace complex that was built by the Umayyad Caliphate in the 10th century. The complex was named after the wife of the caliph Abd al-Rahman III, who commissioned its construction.

Madinat al-Zahra was one of the most important cultural centers in the world during its time. It was home to a library, a school of learning, and a number of workshops where artists and craftsmen produced beautiful works of art.

The complex was abandoned in the 12th century after the fall of the Umayyad Caliphate. It was not until the 19th century that archaeologists began to excavate the site. Today, the ruins of Madinat al-Zahra are a UNESCO World Heritage Site.

The Archaeological Ensemble of Madinat al-Zahra is located about 8 kilometers from Cordoba. It is open from Tuesday to Sunday, and admission is €10.

5.3. Julio Romero de Torres Museum

The Julio Romero de Torres Museum is dedicated to the work of the Spanish painter Julio Romero de Torres (1874-1930). Romero de Torres was born in Cordoba, and he spent most of his life there. He is known for his paintings of beautiful women, often with a religious or mystical theme.

The museum's collection includes over 300 paintings by Romero de Torres. The museum also has a collection of sculptures, drawings, and prints by the artist.

The Julio Romero de Torres Museum is located in the center of Cordoba. It is open from Tuesday to Sunday, and admission is €6.

These are just a few of the many cultural attractions that can be found in Cordoba. With its rich history and culture, Cordoba is a city that has something to offer everyone.

5.4. Flamenco Shows and Performances

There are many opportunities to see flamenco in Cordoba. The city is home to a number of flamenco tablaos, or performance venues. Some of the most popular tablaos include:

Casa del Arte Flamenco: This tablao is located in the heart of the old town, and offers traditional flamenco shows.

Tablao El Cardenal: This tablao is located in a beautiful 16th-century palace, and offers a more sophisticated flamenco experience.

La Carbonería: This tablao is located in a former coal store, and offers a more authentic flamenco experience.

In addition to tablaos, there are also many flamenco performances held in other venues around the city. The city's main theater, the Gran Teatro, often hosts flamenco performances. There are also a number of smaller theaters and concert halls that host flamenco shows.

Traditional Festivals and Events

Cordoba is home to a number of traditional festivals and events throughout the year. Some of the most popular festivals include:

Carnaval de Córdoba: This festival is held in February, and is a lively celebration of music, dance, and costumes.

Semana Santa: This festival is held in April, and is a religious celebration of the Passion of Christ.

Fiesta de los Patios: This festival is held in May, and is a celebration of the city's beautiful patios.

Festival de la Guitarra de Córdoba: This festival is held in July, and is a celebration of the guitar.

These are just a few of the many cultural highlights that Cordoba has to offer. With its rich history and vibrant arts scene, Cordoba is a city that is sure to captivate visitors from all over the world.

In addition to the above, here are some other cultural highlights that you may want to consider:

The Mezquita-Catedral de Córdoba: This UNESCO World Heritage Site is a stunning example of Islamic architecture.

The Alcázar de Córdoba: This Moorish palace is one of the best-preserved examples of its kind in Spain.

The Roman Bridge: This bridge was built in the 1st century AD, and is one of the most iconic landmarks in Cordoba.

The Jewish Quarter: This historic quarter is home to a number of synagogues and other Jewish landmarks.

6. Uncovering Cordoba's Gastronomy

6.1. Local Cuisine and Must-Try Dishes

Here are some of the must-try dishes in Cordoba:

Salmorejo: This cold soup is made with tomato, bread, olive oil, and vinegar. It is often garnished with hard-boiled eggs and chopped ham.

Ajoblanco: This white soup is made with almonds, garlic, bread, olive oil, and vinegar. It is often garnished with grapes.

Pata de cerdo: This dish is made with pork leg that has been slow-cooked in a rich sauce. It is often served with potatoes and vegetables.

Rabo de toro: This dish is made with oxtail that has been slow-cooked in a flavorful sauce. It is often served with potatoes and vegetables.

Carne en salsa: This dish is made with beef that has been cooked in a rich sauce. It is often served with rice or potatoes.

Pescado frito: This dish is made with fried fish. It is often served with a simple sauce of lemon juice and olive oil.

Tortilla de patatas: This Spanish omelet is made with potatoes, onions, and eggs. It is often served with a side of salad or bread.

Churros: These fried dough pastries are often dipped in chocolate sauce. They are a popular snack or dessert.

Mazapán: This almond paste is often made into figurines or other shapes. It is a popular sweet treat in Spain.

6.2. Tapas Culture in Cordoba

Tapas are small, savory dishes that are often served with drinks. They are a popular way to start a meal or to snack on while enjoying a drink with friends. Cordoba has a thriving tapas culture, and there are many great places to try tapas in the city.

Here are some of the best places to try tapas in Cordoba:

Casa Pepe: This restaurant is a Cordoba institution. It has been serving up delicious tapas since 1920.

La Taberna del Guadalquivir: This restaurant is located in the heart of the old town. It has a wide selection of tapas to choose from.

La Cuchara de San Lorenzo: This restaurant is located in the Jewish Quarter. It is known for its traditional Andalusian tapas.

La Abacería: This restaurant is located in the trendy Soho district. It has a modern take on tapas.

La Carbonería: This restaurant is located in the old town. It is known for its grilled meats and seafood.

When trying tapas in Cordoba, there are a few things to keep in mind. First, tapas are typically served in small portions, so it is common to order several different dishes to share. Second, tapas are often priced by the piece, so it is easy to keep your costs under control. Finally, tapas are meant to be enjoyed with a drink, so be sure to order a glass of wine, beer, or sangria to accompany your meal.

Cordoba is a city with a rich and diverse culinary history. The city's tapas culture is a great way to experience the best of Cordoba's cuisine.

6.3. Recommended Restaurants and Cafés

La Taberna del Guadalquivir is a traditional Andalusian restaurant located in the heart of the city. The menu features a variety of tapas, as well as more substantial dishes such as lamb tagines and paella.

La Cuchara de San Lorenzo is a Michelin-starred restaurant that serves modern Andalusian cuisine. The menu changes seasonally, but always features fresh, local ingredients.

Casa Pepe de la Judería is a popular restaurant that serves traditional Jewish cuisine. The menu features dishes such as callos (tripe stew) and albóndigas (meatballs).

El Churrasco Cordobés is a steakhouse that serves up some of the best grilled meats in the city. The menu features a variety of cuts of beef, lamb, and pork, all cooked over an open fire.

La Posada del Potro is a historic inn that has been serving food since the 16th century. The menu features a variety of traditional Andalusian dishes, as well as some more modern options.

6.4. Local Markets and Food Experiences

In addition to its excellent restaurants, Cordoba also has a number of great markets and food experiences. Here are a few of the best:

Mercado Victoria is a large covered market that sells a variety of fresh produce, meats, and cheeses. The market is also home to a number of small restaurants and cafes.

Mercado de la Corredera is a smaller market that specializes in local produce. The market is also home to a number of traditional Andalusian food stalls.

Feria de Abril is a large annual fair that takes place in Cordoba in April. The fair features a variety of food stalls, as well as traditional Andalusian music and dancing.

Here are a few tips for eating in Cordoba:

Try the salmorejo. Salmorejo is a cold soup made with tomato, bread, olive oil, and vinegar. It is a classic Andalusian dish and is a must-try when in Cordoba.

Order a ración. A ración is a small portion of food. This is a great way to try a variety of different dishes without having to commit to a large meal.

Don't forget the tapas. Tapas are small, savory snacks that are served with drinks. They are a great way to start your meal or to have a light snack.

Enjoy the atmosphere. Cordoba is a city with a rich history and culture. Eating in Cordoba is a great way to experience the city and its culture.

7. Day Trips from Cordoba

7.1. Medina Azahara

Medina Azahara was the palace and summer capital of the Umayyad Caliphate in Córdoba. It was built in the 9th century and was one of the most magnificent cities in the world at the time. However, it was sacked and destroyed by Berber tribes in the 11th century. Today, only ruins remain, but they are still impressive and give a glimpse of the city's former glory.

7.2. Sierra de Córdoba

The Sierra de Córdoba is a mountain range located to the north of Córdoba. It is a popular destination for hiking, camping, and mountain biking. The mountains are home to a variety of wildlife, including deer, boars, and eagles. There are also a number of caves and waterfalls in the area.

7.3. Montilla and Montilla-Moriles Wine Region

The Montilla and Montilla-Moriles Wine Region is located to the south of Córdoba. It is one of the oldest wine regions in Spain and is known for its white wines made from the Pedro Ximénez grape. The region is also home to a number of bodegas (wineries) that offer tours and tastings.

7.4. Priego de Córdoba

Priego de Córdoba is a town located to the south of Córdoba. It is known for its whitewashed houses, its beautiful fountains, and its ceramics. The town is also home to a number of churches and convents, including the Convento de Santa Clara, which houses a museum of religious art.

7.5. Ecija

Ecija is a town located to the east of Córdoba. It is known as the "White City" due to its whitewashed houses. The town is also known for its flamenco shows and its tapas bars. Ecija is home to a number of churches and convents, including the Cathedral of Ecija, which is one of the largest cathedrals in Spain.

These are just a few of the many day trips that can be taken from Córdoba. With its rich history and culture, Córdoba is a great base for exploring Andalusia.

8. Outdoor Activities and Natural Wonders in Cordoba

8.1. Guadalquivir River Activities

The Guadalquivir River flows through the heart of Cordoba. The river is a popular spot for swimming, fishing, and boating. There are also several hiking and biking trails that follow the river.

One of the most popular things to do on the Guadalquivir River is to take a boat tour. Boat tours offer a unique perspective of the city and the river. There are several different companies that offer boat tours, so you can choose one that fits your budget and interests.

If you prefer to be more active, you can rent a kayak or canoe and explore the river on your own. There are several different places where you can rent kayaks and canoes.

The Guadalquivir River is also a great place for swimming. There are several different beaches along the river where you can swim. The water is usually very clean and refreshing.

If you're looking for a more challenging activity, you can try hiking or biking along the Guadalquivir River. There are several different trails that follow the river. The trails range in difficulty from easy to difficult, so you can find one that's right for you.

8.2. Exploring the Sierra Morena

The Sierra Morena is a mountain range that lies to the north of Cordoba. The mountains are home to a variety of wildlife, including deer, boars, and eagles. There are also several different hiking and biking trails that wind through the mountains.

One of the most popular things to do in the Sierra Morena is to go hiking. There are several different hiking trails that range in difficulty from easy to difficult. The trails offer stunning views of the mountains and the surrounding countryside.

If you prefer to be more active, you can try biking in the Sierra Morena. There are several different biking trails that wind through the mountains. The trails range in difficulty from easy to difficult, so you can find one that's right for you.

No matter what your interests are, you're sure to find something to enjoy in the Sierra Morena. The mountains offer a variety of outdoor activities and stunning natural beauty.

In addition to the activities listed above, there are many other things to do in and around Cordoba. Here are a few suggestions:

Visit the Mezquita de Córdoba, a UNESCO World Heritage Site.

Explore the Jewish Quarter, a historic district with narrow streets and whitewashed houses.

Take a walk through the Alcazar de Cordoba, a Moorish palace that was once the seat of the Muslim rulers of Cordoba.

Visit the Roman Bridge, a 1st-century bridge that spans the Guadalquivir River.

Enjoy a flamenco show, a traditional Spanish dance that originated in Andalusia.

8.3. Hiking and Nature Walks

There are many great hiking and nature walks to choose from in Cordoba.

Parque Natural Sierra de Hornachuelos: This park is home to a variety of wildlife, including deer, boars, and wolves. There are also several hiking trails that offer stunning views of the surrounding countryside.

Parque de la Sierra Norte: This park is located north of Cordoba and is home to a variety of hiking trails, as well as a lake and a number of picnic areas.

Parque de la Asomada: This park, which lies in the center of Cordoba, has breathtaking views of both the Mezquita and the city. The park also has a number of walking routes that meander around it.

8.4. Botanical Gardens and Parks

Cordoba also has a number of beautiful botanical gardens and parks.

Jardín Botánico de Córdoba: This botanical garden is home to a wide variety of plants from around the world. There are also several greenhouses that house plants from tropical and subtropical climates.

Parque de la Alameda: This park is located in the heart of Cordoba and is a popular spot for locals and tourists alike. There are several fountains, a lake, and a number of benches where you can relax and enjoy the scenery.

Parque de las Delicias: This park is located on the outskirts of Cordoba and is a great place to escape the hustle and bustle of the city. There are several walking trails, a lake, and a number of picnic areas.

No matter what your interests are, you are sure to find something to enjoy in Cordoba. So get out there and explore all that this beautiful city has to offer!

Additional Information

Hiking and Nature Walks:

The best time to go hiking in Cordoba is during the spring or fall, when the weather is mild.

Wear supportive footwear, and pack lots of water and snacks.

If you are planning on hiking in a national park, be sure to get a permit in advance.

Botanical Gardens and Parks:

The best time to visit a botanical garden or park is during the spring or summer, when the plants are in bloom.

Be sure to wear comfortable shoes and bring a hat and sunscreen.

Many botanical gardens and parks offer guided tours, which can be a great way to learn more about the plants and animals that live there.

9. Shopping and Souvenirs in Cordoba

9.1. Traditional Crafts and Artisans

Cordoba has a long tradition of craftsmanship, and there are many artisans in the city who create beautiful and unique items. Some of the most popular traditional crafts include:

Ceramics: Cordoba is known for its beautiful ceramics, which are often decorated with intricate patterns and designs.

Leather goods: Cordoba is also known for its high-quality leather goods, such as bags, wallets, and belts.

Jewelry: Cordoba is home to many talented jewelers who create stunning pieces of jewelry using precious metals and stones.

Furniture: Cordoba has a long tradition of furniture making, and there are many artisans in the city who create beautiful and unique pieces of furniture.

9.2. Shopping Streets and Districts

Cordoba has several shopping streets and districts where you can find a variety of shops selling everything from souvenirs to high-end fashion. Some of the most popular shopping areas include:

Calle del Cardenal Salazar: This pedestrian street is home to a number of shops selling traditional crafts, souvenirs, and gifts.

Calle del Gran Capitán: This street is lined with boutiques selling high-end fashion and accessories.

Mercado Victoria: This covered market is a great place to find fresh produce, meats, cheeses, and other local products.

Zoco de Cordoba: This traditional Arab market is a great place to find souvenirs, spices, and other Middle Eastern goods.

9.3. Souvenir Ideas and Local Products

Here are a few ideas for souvenirs to buy in Cordoba:

Ceramics: A beautiful piece of Cordoba ceramics is a great way to remember your trip.

Leather goods: A high-quality leather bag or wallet is a practical and stylish souvenir.

Jewelry: A piece of jewelry made with precious metals and stones is a beautiful and unique souvenir.

Furniture: A piece of Cordoba furniture is a great way to add a touch of Spanish style to your home.

Local products: There are many delicious local products to choose from, such as olive oil, sherry, and ham.

When shopping in Cordoba, it is important to be aware of the following tips:

Bargain: It is customary to bargain in Cordoba, so don't be afraid to haggle with the shopkeepers.

Shop around: Compare prices before you buy, as you can often find the same item for a lower price at a different shop.

Beware of counterfeit goods: There are many counterfeit goods sold in Cordoba, so be sure to buy from reputable shops.

With a little planning, you can find the perfect souvenirs to remember your trip to Cordoba.

10. Planning Your Itinerary

10.1. One-Day Itinerary

10.1. One-Day Itinerary

If you are only in Cordoba for one day, here is a suggested itinerary:

Start your day with a visit to the Mezquita. This magnificent mosque-cathedral is one of the most impressive buildings in Spain.

After visiting the Mezquita, take a walk through the Jewish Quarter. This historic district is home to narrow streets, whitewashed houses, and charming shops.

In the afternoon, enjoy a traditional Spanish lunch at a tapas bar. Cordoba is known for its delicious tapas, so you are sure to find something to your taste.

In the evening, catch a flamenco show. Flamenco is a traditional Spanish dance that is performed to the accompaniment of guitar and singing.

10.2. Two-Day Itinerary

If you have two days in Cordoba, you can see even more of the city. Here is a suggested itinerary:

Day 1:

Start your day with a visit to the Mezquita.

After visiting the Mezquita, take a walk through the Jewish Quarter.

In the afternoon, visit the Alcazar de los Reyes Cristianos. This impressive palace was built by the

Christian monarchs who conquered Cordoba in the 13th century.

In the evening, enjoy a traditional Spanish dinner at a tapas bar.

Day 2:

Start your day with a visit to the Roman Bridge. This bridge was built by the Romans in the 1st century AD and is one of the most iconic landmarks in Cordoba.

After visiting the Roman Bridge, take a walk through the Alcazar Gardens. These beautiful gardens are located within the Alcazar complex and offer stunning views of the city.

In the afternoon, visit the Museo de Bellas Artes. This museum houses a collection of Spanish art from the 13th to the 20th centuries.

In the evening, enjoy a flamenco show. Flamenco is a traditional Spanish dance that is performed to the accompaniment of guitar and singing.

10.3. Three-Day Itinerary

Day 1:

Start your day with a visit to the Mezquita. This magnificent mosque-cathedral is one of the most impressive buildings in Spain.

After visiting the Mezquita, take a walk through the Jewish Quarter. This historic district is home to narrow streets, whitewashed houses, and charming shops.

In the afternoon, visit the Alcazar de los Reyes Cristianos. This impressive palace was built by the Christian monarchs who conquered Cordoba in the 13th century.

In the evening, enjoy a traditional Spanish dinner at a tapas bar. Cordoba is known for its delicious tapas, so you are sure to find something to your taste.

Day 2:

Start your day with a visit to the Roman Bridge. This bridge was built by the Romans in the 1st century AD and is one of the most iconic landmarks in Cordoba.

After visiting the Roman Bridge, take a walk through the Alcazar Gardens. These beautiful gardens are located within the Alcazar complex and offer stunning views of the city.

In the afternoon, visit the Museo de Bellas Artes. This museum houses a collection of Spanish art from the 13th to the 20th centuries.

In the evening, enjoy a flamenco show. Flamenco is a traditional Spanish dance that is performed to the accompaniment of guitar and singing.

Day 3:

On your last day in Cordoba, you can visit some of the city's other attractions, such as the Capilla de San Bartolomé, the Palacio de Viana, or the Museo Arqueológico.

You can also take a day trip to one of the many nearby towns or villages, such as Medina Azahara or Montoro.

10.4. Week-long Itinerary

Day 1:

Start your day with a visit to the Mezquita. This magnificent mosque-cathedral is one of the most impressive buildings in Spain.

After visiting the Mezquita, take a walk through the Jewish Quarter. This historic district is home to narrow streets, whitewashed houses, and charming shops.

In the afternoon, visit the Alcazar de los Reyes Cristianos. This impressive palace was built by the Christian monarchs who conquered Cordoba in the 13th century.

In the evening, enjoy a traditional Spanish dinner at a tapas bar. Cordoba is known for its delicious tapas, so you are sure to find something to your taste.

Day 2:

Start your day with a visit to the Roman Bridge. This bridge was built by the Romans in the 1st century AD and is one of the most iconic landmarks in Cordoba.

After visiting the Roman Bridge, take a walk through the Alcazar Gardens. These beautiful gardens are located within the Alcazar complex and offer stunning views of the city.

In the afternoon, visit the Museo de Bellas Artes. This museum houses a collection of Spanish art from the 13th to the 20th centuries.

In the evening, enjoy a flamenco show. Flamenco is a traditional Spanish dance that is performed to the accompaniment of guitar and singing.

Day 3:

On your third day in Cordoba, you can visit some of the city's other attractions, such as the Capilla de San Bartolomé, the Palacio de Viana, or the Museo Arqueológico.

You can also take a day trip to one of the many nearby towns or villages, such as Medina Azahara or Montoro.

Day 4:

On your fourth day in Cordoba, you can take a cooking class and learn how to make some of the city's most famous dishes.

In the afternoon, you can visit the Cordoba Cathedral. This beautiful cathedral was built on the site of the former mosque and is a UNESCO World Heritage Site.

In the evening, you can enjoy a traditional Andalusian dinner at a restaurant in the city center.

Day 5:

On your fifth day in Cordoba, you can visit the Medina Azahara. This UNESCO World Heritage

Site is the ruins of a magnificent palace complex that was built by the Umayyad caliphs in the 10th century.

In the afternoon, you can take a walk through the countryside outside of Cordoba. This is a great opportunity to enjoy the beautiful Andalusian landscape.

In the evening, you can enjoy a farewell dinner at a restaurant in the city center.

Day 6:

On your sixth day in Cordoba, you can visit the Museo Julio Romero de Torres. This museum houses a collection of paintings by the famous Spanish artist Julio Romero de Torres.

In the afternoon, you can take a walk through the Parque de la Asuncion. This beautiful park is located in the heart of the city and is a great place to relax and enjoy the outdoors.

Day 7:

On your seventh and final day in Cordoba, you can relax and enjoy your last few hours in the city.

In the afternoon, you can take a taxi or bus to the airport and catch your flight home.

11. Practical Information and Resources

11.1. Useful Contacts and Websites

Tourist Information Office: The tourist information office is located in the Palacio de Congresos y Exposiciones, on Plaza de España. They can provide you with maps, brochures, and information on things to do in Cordoba.

Cordoba City Council: The Cordoba City Council website has a wealth of information on the city, including history, culture, and events.

Cordoba Tourism Board: The Cordoba Tourism Board website has information on things to do in Cordoba, as well as tips on where to stay, eat, and shop.

Cordoba Airport: Cordoba Airport is located 10 kilometers (6 miles) from the city center. There are direct flights from major cities in Spain, as well as from some European cities.

Train Station: The Cordoba train station is located in the city center. There are direct trains from Madrid, Seville, and other major cities in Spain.

Bus Station: The Cordoba bus station is located in the city center. There are direct buses from major cities in Spain, as well as from some European cities.

Taxis: Taxis are readily available in Cordoba. The fare is based on the distance traveled.

Rental Cars: There are several car rental companies located in Cordoba. This is a good option if you want to explore the surrounding area.

11.2. Emergency Numbers

Police: 112

Fire Department: 080

Ambulance: 061

Tourist Information: 957 47 35 00

Additional Information

Currency: The currency in Spain is the euro (€).

Time Zone: Cordoba is in the Central European Time Zone (CET).

Language: The official language of Spain is Spanish. However, English is widely spoken in Cordoba.

Visas: Citizens of most countries do not need a visa to visit Spain for up to 90 days. However, it is always a good idea to check with your local Spanish embassy or consulate for the latest visa requirements.

Weather: Cordoba has a Mediterranean climate with hot, dry summers and mild winters. The average temperature in July is 29°C (84°F) and the average temperature in January is 10°C (50°F).

Getting Around: The best way to get around Cordoba is on foot or by bicycle. The city is relatively small and easy to walk around. There is also a good public transportation system, including buses and taxis.

Accommodation: There are a variety of accommodation options in Cordoba, from budget hostels to luxury hotels.

Food: Cordoba is a foodie's paradise. The city has a wide variety of restaurants serving traditional Andalusian cuisine, as well as international fare.

11.3. Medical Facilities and Pharmacies

Cordoba has a number of medical facilities and pharmacies that can provide care for travelers. The following are some of the most convenient and well-regarded options:

Hospital Universitario Reina Sofía is the main hospital in Cordoba. It is located at Avda. Menéndez Pidal, s/n, 14004 Córdoba, Spain. The hospital has a 24-hour emergency room and a wide range of medical specialists.

Hospital Quirónsalud Córdoba is a private hospital that offers a high level of care. It is located at Avda. de la Mano de Fátima, 1, 14004 Córdoba, Spain. The hospital has a 24-hour emergency room and a wide range of medical specialists.

Clínica Santa Ana is a private hospital that offers a wide range of medical services. It is located at Avda. del Gran Capitán, 10, 14004 Córdoba, Spain. The hospital has a 24-hour emergency room and a wide range of medical specialists.

Farmacia La Trinidad is a pharmacy that is located in the heart of Cordoba. It is open from 9am to 9pm, seven days a week. The pharmacy has a wide range of medications and can also provide medical advice.

Farmacia San Rafael is a pharmacy that is located near the train station. It is open from 9am to 8pm, seven days a week. The pharmacy has a wide range of medications and can also provide medical advice.

If you need medical attention, it is important to seek care as soon as possible. If you are not sure where to go, you can ask your hotel or a local resident for recommendations. You can also call the emergency number 112 for assistance.

In addition to medical facilities, there are a number of resources available for travelers in Cordoba. The following are some of the most helpful resources:

International Association for Medical Assistance to Travelers (IAMAT) provides information and assistance to travelers who need medical care while abroad. The organization has a website that provides information on health risks and travel advisories for specific countries. IAMAT also offers a membership program that provides discounts on medical care and travel insurance.

Spanish National Tourist Office provides information on travel to Spain, including information on health care. The organization has a website that provides information on hospitals, clinics, and pharmacies in Spain. The Spanish National Tourist Office also has a toll-free number that can be used to get information on health care.

Your embassy or consulate can provide information on health care in Spain and can help you to find a doctor or hospital if you need medical attention.

It is important to be prepared for any medical emergencies that may occur while traveling. You should pack a first-aid kit that includes bandages, antibiotic ointment, pain relievers, and motion sickness medication. You should also make sure that you have a valid passport and travel insurance.

Conclusion

As we reach the end of our journey through the pages of "Cordoba Spain Travel Guide 2023: Essential Pocket Guide," we hope that you have been inspired to embark on an adventure of a lifetime in this enchanting city. Cordoba is not just a destination; it is an immersive experience that will ignite your senses, touch your heart, and leave you with lasting memories.

In Cordoba, history breathes, culture thrives, and authenticity permeates every corner. From the awe-inspiring Mezquita-Catedral to the vibrant streets of the Jewish Quarter, every step you take reveals a tapestry woven with stories of resilience, diversity, and the unbreakable spirit of the people who call this city home.

We have shared with you the insider tips, local insights, and must-visit recommendations that will ensure you make the most of your time in Cordoba. Whether you find yourself exploring the historical landmarks, indulging in the tantalizing flavors of the local cuisine, or immersing yourself in the vibrant traditions and festivals, our guide has equipped you with the knowledge to create an authentic and unforgettable experience.

But beyond the practicalities, Cordoba offers something intangible—an invitation to connect with the essence of Spain, to embrace the beauty of cultural fusion, and to be touched by the warmth of the Cordoban people. It is a city that invites you to slow down, to savor the moments, and to appreciate the rich tapestry of life that unfolds before you.

As you bid farewell to Cordoba, carry with you the memories of vibrant flamenco performances, the taste of traditional dishes, the echoes of ancient whispers in the narrow streets, and the undeniable feeling that you have been a part of something extraordinary. Allow the spirit of Cordoba to continue inspiring you long after your journey ends.

We extend our deepest gratitude to the people of Cordoba who have graciously shared their stories, insights, and hospitality. Their passion for their city has illuminated our path, and we hope it does the same for you.

So, with a sense of fulfillment and a heart filled with the spirit of Cordoba, we invite you to take the leap, to embrace the allure of this remarkable city, and to embark on a transformative journey that will forever hold a cherished place in your memories.

Thank you for joining us on this adventure. May your travels be filled with discovery, joy, and the magic that awaits in every corner of Cordoba.

¡Buen viaje y hasta pronto! (Safe travels and see you soon!)

Printed in Great Britain
by Amazon

41644943R00086